# KRAV MAGA:
## PRINCIPLES & TECHNIQUES

DEVIN SHIRLEY

D1303090

Copyright © 2020 Devin Shirley

All rights reserved.

ISBN: 979-8-6905-0708-4

Editing: Melissa Runyon, Brooke Crump, Nikki Ackerman
Photos: Stacy Cox
Cover design: Jeremy Shirley

*This book is dedicated to*

*My family for giving up countless hours for me to pursue my passion to train, teach, and run the training center.*

*The many students who have allowed me the privilege and opportunity to train them.*

# CONTENTS

# ACKNOWLEDGMENTS

Melissa Runyon, Brooke Crump, and Nikki Ackerman for reviewing and editing this book.  You helped me to bring a more cohesive thought process and a level of communication I would not have achieved on my own

Stacy Cox, for making the time and exerting the effort it took to not only photograph, but also to review and edit hundreds of images.  Your photos and sustained energy through the hours of photo shoots kept us focused

Jeremy Shirley, for creating the awesome cover that captures the essence of the book.  You always do great graphic work for me and literally within just a few hours you are able to produce a great product. Not to mention you are a great little brother.

Ann Marie Gibbs, for opening the next Krav Fit training center and supporting the work we do – I am truly thankful to you for carrying on the vision.

Arny Ferrando, for being a faithful and longtime Krav Maga practitioner, instructor, friend, and fellow member of the long gray line.

Joe Huskey, for remaining my friend and fellow Krav Maga practitioner and instructor.  Without your support, we never would have made it as far as we did.  I am truly grateful for your dedication, sacrifice, and commitment through all these years.  Thank you for giving me the leg up I needed to make the dream a reality.

And many thanks to all the Krav Fit staff through the years for their selfless commitment to training students and committing to their own training.  None of it would have been possible without you.

# INTRODUCTION

Welcome to the level 1, yellow belt curriculum for Krav Maga within the Krav Fit organization. Hopefully, you have picked up this manual because you are interested in learning how to defend yourself in a variety of situations. This manual is the first step to making you safer, more aware, and more confident. And, hopefully, you will get in better shape and have fun along the way.

As you begin your training, understand that at its core, Krav Maga is a principle based system. Yes, there are certain techniques, but those techniques have their roots within the principles of Krav Maga. And, because Krav Maga is an open system, the techniques may change over time as situations, attacks, and scenarios change. However, the principles of the system do not change. So, while we present to you these techniques, know that you do not have to perform them perfectly to be successful. The better you perform them, the better and more effective at defending yourself you will be, but you don't have to be the ultimate Krav Maga practitioner for them to work.

We do test students on this material after they have trained in these techniques for a while. How long it takes you to become proficient is dependent on you – how frequently you train, the quality of your training, and your own capabilities, as well as your motivation and commitment to continually get better. Some people can learn and do the material well in a matter of months; others may take a year. It doesn't matter. What matters is can you perform what you learn when it counts, when the attacker grabs you or shoves a gun in your face. That is the true test of whether you can effectively defend yourself.

Keep in mind, what we present in this manual are principles and techniques, but the real value is in the training you receive. You need to train realistically and without sustaining injuries to maximize the training benefit and to get the most out of what this manual presents. We encourage you to find someone to train with, preferably a certified instructor who knows what they are doing. However, if no instructor or training center is available, use the material, train with a friend, following the description of the techniques, and training under a variety of situational occurrences. If you have questions in regards to these techniques, we want to know. You can email info@kravfit.us, and we will respond to your questions. We hope to have videos soon of these techniques that you can use for reference as well. When we do, we will publish those.

Now, let's get to it.

# CHAPTER 1

# STANCE

## Stance

There are two basic stances in Krav Maga – Neutral Stance and Fight Stance. Let's start by first describing the Fight Stance.

### Fight Stance

The Fight Stance allows us to be ready for an attack and to initiate strikes if the situation requires it, while still allowing us the potential to de-escalate if possible. The Fight Stance is the stance we go to once we have recognized we are being attacked or an attack is imminent. It is our ready position, preparing us to respond appropriately to an attack.

Your feet should be a comfortable distance apart. To do this, place your feet about shoulder width apart and take a natural step forward (right handed defenders, step with your left foot forward, left handed defenders step with your right foot forward).

If you are too wide or too narrow, you could inhibit or slow down your movement or simply be less balanced in your stance.

Weight distribution is important in the fight stance as well. You should place slightly more weight on the forward foot, with approximately 60% on the forward foot and 40% on the back foot. Your back heel should be raised off the ground a little. This will help you keep your weight forward and also give you the ability to move by pushing off the ball of your rear foot.

Legs should be slightly bent at the knees and remain flexible in the fight stance position. This ensures you are able to respond quickly and efficiently to any movement requirements.

Your torso and legs should be mostly squared up with your attacker. While a traditional bladed stance or "L" stance may provide more protection, it may inhibit your ability to deliver some strikes and counters more effectively. So, we like to stay squared up towards our opponent to give us more options for blocking and countering quickly and effectively.

Hands are positioned in front of your face with the fingers relaxed, and a comfortable distance in front of the face, with your elbows in to protect your ribs.

This primary position is what we use when we know we are in a fight or about to be in one. Our Fight Stance allows us to be in a complete ready state so we can quickly engage and neutralize an opponent.

## Neutral Stance

The Neutral or Passive Stance is any relaxed or non-ready position you may be in. Simply put, it can be any position that is not the Fight Stance.

# CHAPTER 2

# MOVEMENT

## Movement

When we move in Krav Maga, we want to do it in a way that minimizes any imbalance we may have in our movement. When you move, there is always a point at which you will only have one foot on the ground while the other one is off the ground, moving in the direction you are headed. When this happens you have a moment of imbalance where your body is relying on only one foot to hold you up. If you look at a natural stride, you will have an even greater moment of imbalance at the moment the lifted foot passes beside the foot on the ground because you now have a narrow stance where you cannot quickly recover if you were to trip or get pushed.

So, to help alleviate this issue of imbalance with a natural walking movement, we address the issue of our feet passing beside each other.

In your Fight Stance, to move effectively while maintaining a better sense of balance, you first move the foot that is in the direction you want to go. For instance, if you want to move forward, you first step with the forward foot. If you want to move backward, your first step is with the back foot. If you step laterally to the right, you step first with the right foot. If you step laterally left, you step with the left foot first. This same concept applies if you step forward diagonally or backward diagonally.

## Stepping Forward

*Start in Fight Stance*　　　*Step forward with front foot*　　　*Step forward with back foot*

## Stepping Backward

*Start in Fight Stance*　　　*Step backward with back foot*　　　*Step backward with front foot*

## *Stepping Right*

*Start in Fight Stance*     *Step right with right foot*     *Step right with left foot*

## *Stepping Left*

*Start in Fight Stance*     *Step left with left foot*     *Step left with right foot*

After you have taken the first step, you then will see that you are in a widened stance. To narrow the stance, merely bring the other foot with you, moving it approximately the same distance you did with your first step. After you do this, you should be back in your normal fight stance.

This movement is what we refer to as "open – close" with the feet. You will notice that while we still have to lift a foot off the ground to move, we quickly put it back down minimizing the time of imbalance, and we completely avoid having to cross our feet.

*Widened Fight Stance (open)*          *Regular Fight stance (close)*

When you start from a neutral stance, you can choose which foot to start with in your forward movement. After that initial movement, you should then be in a fight stance and move with the appropriate footwork.

Again, the basic concept of moving in Krav Maga is that we move quickly and efficiently without giving up our balance. We close the distance by using the open-close movement of the feet.

# CHAPTER 3

# STRIKING

## Striking

Striking an opponent is required in Krav Maga. To defend yourself effectively, at some point in the defense, you will need to neutralize your opponent in order to stop them from continuing their attacks. In Krav Maga, we use strikes in various ways: sometimes as our initial defense or counterattack and simultaneously (or as close to simultaneous as we are able) with a self-defense technique. To that end, Krav Maga has a variety of methods and strikes we use to help us achieve these goals.

When considering strikes, one of the determining factors for which strike to use is the distance we are from the attacker. We have three basic categories for classifying distance: long range, mid-range, and short range. For long range strikes, we use the longest limbs we have, our legs. For mid-range, we make use of our arms and hands. For short range strikes, we use knees, elbows, and head butts.

Let's start by looking at our mid-range weapons, the arms and hands, which happen to be our most basic form of striking.

### *Straight Punches*
Straight punches are one of the most basic strikes in Krav Maga. In fact, they're probably the most basic strike in any fighting system and is a strike that comes very naturally to us when fighting or defending ourselves. We're just going to take that natural inclination to use our hands and arms and hone it to become an effective weapon in a fight or defense scenario.

To deliver a straight punch from the fight stance, you reach out to your intended target, keeping your elbow down for as long as you are able, allowing it to come up at the last possible second of the punch. To help you train this, think of trying to hold a towel under your arm until the last second.

As you reach out, rotate your hips and shoulders. Doing this ensures two things: 1) you get more reach out of your punch, and 2) you get more power out of your punch. The power comes from the fact you are using your body to punch and not your arms. When you put your whole body into the punch as compared to just your arm, you can get more power out of it. Using simple physics, you can increase the force you exert by either increasing the mass or the acceleration of the object delivering the force or by increasing both mass and acceleration. By rotating the hips and shoulders, you are adding more mass behind your punch, and therefore, are directly increasing the force of the strike. And, by the way, if you increase the acceleration of your punch, with the added mass, you increase the force of your punch even more. So, make sure you are rotating your hips and shoulders as you throw the punch to ensure you get the maximum effect from your strike.

To make a fist when you punch, curl your fingers in toward your palm and lay your thumb across the curled fingers.

As you strike the target, the first two knuckles at the base of the first two fingers should strike the target, protecting your smaller fingers and wrist from injury.

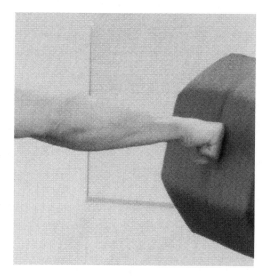

Remember, punching is one of our most basic defenses and can be used in a variety of situations to help you neutralize an attacker. You can maximize the effectiveness of the punch by following the principles outlined above.

## Left/Right Combination

Once we attack someone, we want to continue our attacks until we have neutralized our assailant. So, we should not throw only one punch. We should learn to punch in combination with other punches and strikes. The left/right (or jab/cross) is the first of many combinations. We will cover the rest in later material.

When throwing a jab/cross combination, you start with the hand of the leading leg to punch (jab), using the principles described above in the previous section on Straight Punches. When you recoil the jab, that is the moment you begin the punch with the hand of the back leg (cross). The basic concept is that your hands should meet halfway between, so that as your front hand is coming back, your back hand passes it on its way out to the intended target. The best way to think of this is by imagining you are pulling a rope with both hands around your neck. As one punch is thrown, it pulls the other hand back to recoil.

The jab/cross combination is the most basic punch combination and can be easily performed using the basic principles of straight punches and allows you to provide continuous and effective attacks against an assailant.


## Straight Punch with Advance

Fights are not static. In fact, you should be moving in a fight if you want to maximize your protection and your effectiveness in striking. Movement can be forward, back, sideways, at an angle, etc. For now, let's focus on moving forward.

When you punch, say with the left punch first, you advance in with your left foot. Your left foot should land on the ground about the same time as your punch lands on the target.

Doing this helps to maximize your power. You should not try to land your punch while your foot is in the air. The punch will be less powerful, and you could end up in a situation where you get caught off balance.

As your left punch recoils, you can bring the rear foot forward to return to your normal fight stance. Notice that the footwork is the same as the Open-Close principle we described in the Movement section.

Now, you can add in the right punch to make a left/right combination while advancing. To do this, throw the right punch as your left punch recoils, all while advancing in with your feet. Just as the left punch struck the target at about the same time as the left foot landed on the ground, the right punch should strike the target about the same time as the right foot lands on the ground.

## *Straight Punch with Retreat*

When we advance in with an advancing punch, we can close the distance between our attacker and us. While this is what we want, there are times we need to create distance between us and the attacker as well. To do this, we take a step backward using the Open-Close principle of movement for moving backward.

As we move out, we throw a jab, allowing us to send a strike even though we are stepping away, which can deter the attacker from advancing in towards us.

The retreat and countermovement can be used in conjunction with the advance so we can advance in, throw our strikes, and then retreat out to a safe position. How many punches you deliver while in close to the attacker is based on what you feel you can do at that moment. Sometimes it may be more, sometimes it may be less.

## *Straight Punch Low*

When striking with punches, you may not always want to strike the face, and you may want to change target areas. One of the targets you can strike is the stomach or mid-section of the attacker. To do this, you will have to adjust your height, without sacrificing by opening yourself up to other types of attacks.

To perform the straight punch low, we will still maintain the same body mechanics of punching while rotating the hips and shoulders. However, we will drop the height of our punch to change the target. To drop the height, we perform a squat from within our fight stance and punch with either the left or right hand.

As you punch, raise your shoulder up to protect your head. It will help protect against any punches that are thrown at you while you throw your punch.

Once you deliver the punch, stand back up to deliver the next strike.

Should you throw more than one low punch at a time? It depends on the situation and the attacker. If you do deliver more than one low punch, you should ensure you change head and body positions, so the two punches are not delivered from the same static position.

## Palm Strike

The Palm Strike is a variation on the straight punch, using the heel of your palm to strike instead of a fist.

One of the advantages of using the palm strike is reducing the risk of injury to your hands and wrist. You can deliver just as powerful of a strike with the palm as you can a fist.

The body mechanics for the palm strike are the same as those for the straight punches. The only difference is the hand position and striking surface of the hand. To punch with the palm strike, extend your fingers while rotating your hand in at about a 45° angle.

Pull your fingers back as much as possible to keep your fingers from getting injured.

Again, the palm strike is one of the variations you can make to a regular straight punch.

## Eye/Throat Strike

The eye/throat strike is yet another variation of the straight punch with the goal of the strike being to take out a more specific target: the eyes or the throat.

The body mechanics of the eye/throat strike are the same as those for the straight punches and palm strikes. The difference is the hand position and striking surface of the hand. To perform the eye/throat strike, lengthen your fingers out, turning your palm toward the ground.

You want your hand to rotate to about a 45° angle to ensure a greater chance of hitting your intended target, especially if the target is the eyes. If you leave your hand vertical, you take the chance of missing the eyes if you are too far left or right. If the hand is horizontal, you risk missing the eyes if you are too far up or down. With the throat, this may not be the case. You may, in fact, do more of a strike with the hand horizontal, depending on the opening you have to hit your target.

The trickiest part of the eye/throat strike is the striking surface of the hands. You want to strike with a point just behind the tips of your fingers. This will help protect against jamming or breaking your fingers.

You can further prevent injury to the fingers by spacing your fingers only slightly apart or placing them together. If you have too large of a space between fingers, you run the risk of injuring your fingers when you strike your target.

*Fingers Opened*

*Fingers Closed*

The eye/throat strike is a useful tool if you are trying to strike a specific target on your assailant. These targets will require more accurate striking; however, if done right, they can cause significant problems for your assailant.

*Eye Strike*          *Throat Strike*

# CHAPTER 4

# HAMMERFIST PUNCHES

## Hammerfist

Hammerfist punches are another variety of punches that you can use when you're a medium distance from the attacker, and you need to use a mid-range strike. Where straight punches use the flat surface of the fist as its striking surface, the hammerfist punch uses the little finger side of the fist. So, it derives its name from using your fist like a hammer when throwing the punch. While there can be multiple directions and angles for delivering the punch, we will focus on three fundamental forms: Forward, Side, and Downward.

### *Forward*

The forward hammerfist is used from the fight stance and follows the same basic body mechanics of a straight punch - employing the rotation of the hips and shoulders to generate maximum power and effectiveness. We are still aiming for the same target as we would with a straight punch, focusing on the soft areas of the head (face, nose, eyes, mouth, etc.).

As you rotate your hips and shoulders, make a fist and send your arm out as though you were swinging a hammer.

As you reach the target, rotate your fist so that you strike the target area with the side of your fist.

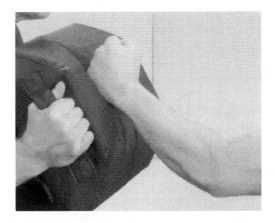

You can use the front or back hand to deliver the hammerfist punch. Like a straight punch, the back hand will deliver a stronger strike, but as long as you are using your hips and shoulders to punch, either side can prove effective. You can also use the hammerfist in a jab/cross combination. So, if you feel the front hand is not as strong for an attack as you would like, you can quickly follow with a backhand hammerfist to deliver a stronger, second strike.

## Side

Hammerfist to the side is a very useful punch when someone is attacking you from the side, and you don't have time to face them before they reach you. This punch will also allow you to strike an attacker as you turn to face them, putting you in a better position to defend and counter with other strikes.

Starting from a neutral stance, first recognize an attack approaching from your side You bring both hands up as if you were about to get into a fight stance.

As your hands come up, raise your elbow as you are turning to face the attacker. Ensure that your head is tucked behind your arm. Note that by raising the elbow you are also giving yourself a way to defend if the attacker is coming at you with a punch. You can use your arm to defend his strike and then counter with your other hand.

As you near the completion of your turn, strike with your hand by extending your arm at the elbow and striking the target with the side of your fist, palm side facing towards the ground.

 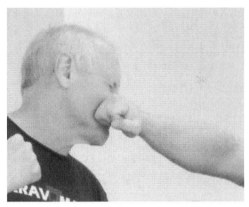

Once you have delivered the hammerfist to the side, you can use other strikes to continue neutralizing your attacker.

## Downward

Use the downward hammerfist in a more specific situation where the target is at or just above your waist level. The concept is the same as that of the hammerfist forward. The big difference is the angle of the strike will be straight down instead of in front of you. An example target is the back of someone's neck as they are doubled over in front of you.

As you strike down, you can do a slight rotation with your hip and shoulder, but the primary focus should be on dropping your weight. To drop your weight, just perform a slight squat. It is the drop of your weight that helps you generate the power for this strike.

As you drop your weight, bring your fist down in front of you toward the intended target and strike with the side of your fist, just as you did with the other hammerfist strikes.

# CHAPTER 5

# ELBOW STRIKES

## Elbow Strikes

In close range, we use elbow strikes against our attacker. If for some reason the attacker has managed to close the distance and get closer to us than we want them, we can use the elbow to deliver an effective strike to either neutralize an attacker or force them to get away.

You can strike a variety of targets with the elbow depending on the position of your body relative to the attacker and if you are in a fight or neutral stance. To deal with this variety of scenario elbows in Krav Maga are broken down into seven basic strikes. The first three elbows deal with striking in the horizontal plane, while the other four deal with striking in the vertical plane.

### *Elbow #1*

Elbow #1 is the simplest and most basic elbow you can use. In fact, the principles for striking with this elbow are the same as striking with a straight punch.

From a fight stance, use the hip and shoulder rotation to generate power for this strike. Raise your elbow up as you start the rotation with your body and strike the target with the point just below your elbow.

Upon striking the target, ensure your momentum is moving in a straight line to, and through, your target. If you move in a circular motion, you may scrape or miss the attacker instead of delivering a robust and direct hit.

Immediately recover the elbow to help protect your body against any other attacks once you've struck your attacker. You can deliver the elbow with the same advancing movement you used in the straight punch with advance, and you can use it in combination with another elbow.

## Elbow #2

Use Elbow #2 when an attacker approaches you from the side, and you don't have time to turn to face them. It is similar in concept to hammerfist from the side but used when a target is in close range, whereas the hammerfist is used when a target is a medium range distance from you.

Since the target is approaching from the side, we will assume you were not expecting the attack and are, therefore, in a neutral stance and not able to turn in time to face the attacker. Once you recognize the attacker is approaching, raise both arms to where your hands are in front of your face.

Then, using the elbow that is on the same side as the attacker, strike the target with the point just above your elbow.

Shift your weight to the side facing the attacker to add more power to your strike. If you recognize the attack too late, you may not be able to effectively shift your weight before they are on top of you. However, you can still throw a good elbow to stop their momentum.

To maximize the power of your elbow, ensure you deliver the strike while moving your elbow in a horizontal plane. Doing so puts all of your force moving toward the attacker. You can move it up in a diagonal movement, but it may not be as strong of a counter.

Once you have delivered the elbow strike, begin turning toward the attacker, continuing with multiple strikes (hammerfist, straight punch, knees, kicks, etc.)

## Elbow #3

Use Elbow #3 when the attacker approaches you from behind. Again, we will assume you are in a neutral stance and did not have a chance to turn before the attacker got close to you. It doesn't matter which elbow you strike with if the attacker is lined up with your centerline. If they are more to your right, use your right elbow. If they are more to your left, use your left elbow. If you don't have a chance to recognize which one to use, just pick a side and use it with everything you've got.

To throw the elbow, bring your hands up to your face and then immediately send the elbow to your intended target while rotating your torso in the same direction you are throwing the elbow.

As you rotate your torso, pivot on the opposite side foot to add power to your strike and make it easier to rotate.

Once you have struck the target, continue turning toward the attacker while delivering multiple counterattacks.

## Elbow #4

With elbow #4, we will start striking in the vertical plane. With this elbow, we assume the attacker is behind us, standing extremely close. The target area for this elbow is the solar plexus area. Assuming you are in a neutral stance, aggressively raise one of your elbows up and back while simultaneously rotating your hips toward the attacker. The hip rotation will add extra power to your strike.

Once you've delivered the elbow, turn to face the attacker and continue delivering more counterattacks.

## Elbow #5

For Elbow #5, the attacker is approaching from behind, but we see that we have an available target- their face.

To deliver this strike, slightly drop your weight by bending your knees and then aggressively drive up with your legs while sharply bringing your elbow up in a vertical plane and back toward the attacker's face or chin.

The striking surface should be the point just above your elbow.

Once you deliver the strike, immediately turn and continue attacking.

## *Elbow #6*

With Elbow #6, the attacker is in front of you, and you are already in your fight stance.

To deliver this elbow, slightly drop your weight by bending your knees and then aggressively drive up with your legs while sharply bringing your elbow up in a vertical plane up and in towards the attacker's face or chin. The striking surface should be the point just below your elbow.

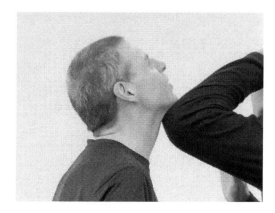

Once you deliver the strike, use multiple counters to continue the attack until you have neutralized the threat.

## Elbow #7

The scenario for Elbow #7 is where the attacker has doubled over in front of you, say from a strike that you delivered such as a groin kick or a knee. While they are doubled over, they expose a target, such as the back of their neck. The situation is very similar to the hammerfist downward strike, where the target is at or just above your waist level.

As you strike down, you can do a slight rotation with your hip and shoulder, but, like the hammerfist downward strike, the main focus should be on dropping your weight. To drop your weight, just perform a squat. It is the weight drop that helps you to generate the power for this strike.

As you drop your weight, bring either arm (whichever is most pertinent based on your angle with the target) with your elbow pointed down toward the intended target and strike with the point just above your elbow.

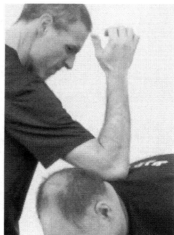

Once you deliver the strike, if the attacker has not gone to the ground, continue with more counters as necessary.

# CHAPTER 6

# KICKS & KNEES

## Kicks

While punches serve as a strike you can use at a mid-range distance, kicks provide us the ability to strike from a longer range. There are various options we can use for kicking a target, depending on the target we want to strike, the angle of attack we want to use and what openings we are provided. This chapter reviews some of the kicks we use in the Krav Maga system.

### Front Kick to the Groin

Front kick to the groin is one of the most basic kicks we have in Krav Maga. This kick is a long-range weapon we can use to help neutralize an attacker. You can deliver this kick from either a neutral stance or fight stance. The target area is the groin, but to help you maximize your power imagine the target is the top of the head and you are just getting there by going through the groin.

To throw this kick, you begin by raising your kicking leg (in a fight stance, using your back leg will be stronger than using your front leg). As you raise your leg, push your hips forward into the kick to generate more power. Also, ensure your knee goes beyond the groin. Where your knee goes, your power will go.

As you raise your leg, snap your foot out to extend to the groin, striking with the shoelace area of your foot. You can also strike with any point along the shin as well, depending on the distance you are from the attacker. The closer you are, the higher up the shin the strike will be, but if you are farther away, it will be the shoelace area of the foot.

When you recoil the kick, ensure you recoil quickly and return your leg to the starting position. You can also choose to land forward on your kicking leg if the attacker is far enough back to successfully do so.

## Round Kick

The Round Kick provides you another long-range weapon you can use against an attacker, but allows you to strike at a different angle and target than the front kick. You can use the round kick to effectively strike anywhere from the knee to the ribs. Typically, you will use it when you are in your fight stance, although it can be performed from a neutral stance.

To deliver the Round Kick, you begin by raising the leg just as you did with the Front Kick to the groin.

*Fight Stance*

*Lifting Knee*

As you raise the leg, begin to rotate your hips and shoulder over toward the intended target, driving your knee past the target. Again, where your knee goes, your power goes. As you rotate your hips, pivot on the foot that is on the ground (called your base foot) about 90 degrees. Doing so will help you rotate your hips and keep you from injuring your knee.

As your knee passes the target, snap your foot out, extending the leg to strike the target. The striking surface should be along the shin or the shoelace area of your foot, depending on your distance from your opponent.

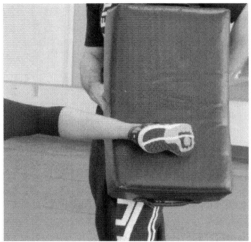

You can deliver the round kick at different angles, depending on the target. For the basic round kick, keep your kick horizontal, striking the ribs. If you were to strike the knees of your opponent, you would angle downward with the round kick. So, the angle of the kick will change with the location of the target area on the attacker.

*Round kick to the knee*

After you deliver the round kick, recoil back into your fight stance. If the tactical situation allows, you can also land forward on your kicking leg.

*Recoil back*                    *Land on forward leg*

## Front Kick to a Vertical Target

This front kick is done similar to front kick to the groin but allows you to strike a different target area on the attacker. In this case, the target is in the area of the midsection, about where the belly button is located or where a belt buckle would be. This kick is an offensive kick, and you should think of it as though you were punching with the foot.

To throw this kick, you begin by raising your kicking leg.

As you raise your leg, punch your hips, along with your leg and foot, towards the target, striking the target area with the ball of your foot.

After you deliver the kick, recoil the leg back into your fight stance.

## Defensive Front Kick

The Defensive Front kick is done similar to front kick to a vertical target, but has a different purpose and striking area. Execute the defensive front kick from a defensive posture with the idea that you are trying to create space between you and the attacker, whereas the front kick to a vertical target is an offensive front kick with the intent to disable or cause pain to the attacker. The target area for the Defensive Front kick is the chest area. By striking the chest area, you will drive the attacker away from you.

To deliver the defensive front kick, raise your kicking leg in the same way you did on the front kick to a vertical target.

As you raise your leg, punch your hips, along with your leg and foot, towards the target, striking the target area with the heel of your foot as you pull your toes back toward you.

After you deliver the kick, recoil the leg back into your fight stance.

## Knees

Knees are one of the close-range weapons we have in Krav Maga. This strike is a devastating strike to use when you are in close with the attacker. A knee can be delivered powerfully to many different target areas such as the midsection, groin, ribs, and head.

To throw this strike, you begin by grabbing the attacker with one arm pinned against the attacker's collarbone, and your hand grabs their shirt or skin, while the other hand grabs the same side arm around the elbow or tricep.

Ensure you keep your elbow below the attacker's shoulder. Doing so allows you to feel the attacker's movements and will help prevent them doing a takedown by building a barrier between you and the attacker.

As your hands control the attacker, raise the leg that you will be using to deliver the knee. (in a fight stance, using your back leg will be stronger than using your front leg).

As you raise your knee, push your hips forward and in to generate more power. When you strike with your knee, ensure you are driving through the target. Pull the attacker toward your knee with your hands as you are driving your knee into the target to ensure you maximize the striking force.

Pull back the leg that delivered the knee and strike again until you neutralize your attacker.

The target area can vary based on your positioning and the position of the target area.

*Knee to mid-section*                    *Knee to head*

# CHAPTER 7

# CONTROL POSITIONS

## Control Positions

When we are in a fight or defense situation, there is a point in time where you have to take control of the attacker or the situation. In this chapter, we review some of the basic control positions to help us better control the attacker and our position relative to the attacker to set enable us to manipulate the attacker's movements and/or set us up to deliver counterattacks.

### *Basic Takedown Defense (Framing)*

Framing is one of the most basic defenses we have when the attacker attempts to perform a takedown by taking out your legs or going for your waist. This basic defense is similar to the position we move to when preparing to throw a knee at the attacker, but in this instance, we will use the stance as a defense against the takedown. The idea behind this defense is that we build a wall between the attacker and the defender while gaining control of the attacker and the situation. In this attack, assume a worst-case scenario where you are not prepared for the attack and are in your neutral or passive stance.

When the attacker makes his move to do the takedown, drop your weight down with your feet moving to a modified fight stance position, where they are a little wider apart, and further back from the attacker in a based-out position.

As you drop your weight, bring your hands up, with your forearm making contact with the attacker's collarbone/neck area, while the other hand grabs hold of the arm on the same side the forearm is defending.

From this position, you have pulled your feet and hips out of the way of the attacker, making it more difficult for him to do a takedown by grabbing your legs or around the waist. Additionally, you have built a wall with your forearm to help you hinder his movement forward. All the while, you are controlling one of his arms.

From here you are in better control to avoid the takedown and begin throwing counters, such as knees.

## Muay Thai Clinch

Another way to defend and control against a takedown is to perform a variation of the framing technique. With the Muay Thai clinch, you follow the same steps as mentioned for framing. However, instead of controlling with your hands and arms on the same side of the attacker's head, you place on arm on either side of their head.

In this instance, place the blade edge of your forearms against the neck of the attacker, while your hands are placed on the back of the attacker's head, one hand covering the other. Ensure you apply pressure with your hands to force the attacker's head down, giving you more control.

 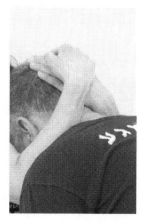

And, just as you did with the basic framing technique, you throw counters from this position. You can also easily rotate the attacker from this position by spinning on your centerline while maintaining the control position.

# CHAPTER 8

# DEFENDING PUNCHES

## Punch Defenses

In a fight, you may experience various punches from your attacker. Therefore, it is imperative to learn to defend against these different punches. When you train these punch defenses, ensure you train them individually at first to focus the correct defense to each one. As you feel more comfortable with the accuracy and speed of your defense, have the attacker mix up the various punches so you learn to read and respond appropriately when you cannot predict which punch the attacker delivers. To make it even more challenging, both you and your attacker should move around while practicing these defenses.

### 360° Defense

We use 360° defenses against punches that are approaching us from outside our hand position. As the name suggests, this defense provides us a 360° protection against any angle of punches coming at us.

It is a direct block to an incoming strike and can be made by merely bending the elbow to form a 90° angle with our arm and to block the incoming strike with the blade edge of our forearms.

Fingers should be fully extended when defending so you can maximize the length of your arm and ensure you have the most protection against the strike. Ideally, you should defend the attack wrist to wrist, but it is possible to defend with any part of the arm from the elbow to the fingertips.

As you execute this defense, you should put the weight of your body into the defense to make it strong and effective against the attack. You can burst toward the attack if possible to get more force behind your defense.

Using the method described above, we can now apply this defense to seven basic positions we use to provide us the full circle of defense.

*Position #1* – Defending an attack coming down directly over your head. Position your arm directly above and just forward of your head.

*Position #2* – Defending an attack coming down and at an angle. Position your arm so that your upper arm is at a position between parallel and perpendicular to the ground.

*Position #3* – Defending an attack coming in directly from the side. Position your arm so that your upper arm is parallel to the ground.

*Position #4* – Defending an attack coming up and at an angle towards the ribs. Position your arm so that your elbow is in toward your body, forming a sort of "w" with your arm.

*Position #5* – Defending an attack coming up and at an angle towards the ribs. It is the same attack as for #4, but this is an alternative defense where you point your hand towards the ground and have your elbow up.

*Position #6* – Defending an attack coming up at an angle. Position your arm so that it is at a position lower than that for #5. If you were to position both arms for this defense, you would form a "v" with your arms. Lock your legs back in this position, as the same defense can be used to defend an upward stab with a knife.

*Position #7* – Defending an attack coming straight up to the body. Position your arm so that your forearm is low and parallel to the ground with your elbow up. Just as with position #6, your legs should be locked out and back.

## Inside Defense vs. Straight Punch

There are a few ways to defend a punch coming straight at your head. One way is to deflect the blow by using a redirecting movement known as the Inside Defense. Use this defense when we are redirecting the punch toward the inside of our body and off the line of attack toward our head. This movement is one of the easier movements to perform in the Krav Maga system.

For this defense, we are going to assume you are in a fight stance with your hands up. When the punch comes from the attacker, redirect the punch off the line of attack using the hand that is on the same side as the attacker's punching hand. Your fingers should be up so that the palm of your hand can make contact with the wrist or arm of the attacker.

Your hand should be angled slightly out and moving in a line that is somewhat away from the body.

As you redirect the punch, your head should move the opposite direction of your hand. Think of tucking your chin to your shoulder. Doing that further ensures you get your head out of the way of the punch. So, if you miscalculate the timing or distance of the redirection, the movement of your head works as a secondary defense.

Once you have defended, you can recoil your hand back to your regular fight stance position, so you are ready for the next attack. It is possible to attack with counters off of this defense, but we will discuss the counters in the level 2 manual.

As a side note, you can also use this defense if you happen to misjudge where the punch is going or if the attacker changes his attack midway through the punch. For instance, if the attacker punches at the head and makes a slight change to hit a little lower than your head, you can then use the same redirecting movement to defend, but now instead of using the palm of your hand to redirect, you will use your forearm.

## Inside Defense vs. Low Straight Punch

When the straight punch is intended for a lower target, such as your midsection, you can modify the regular inside defense to redirect this punch. To perform this defense, use the same side as the attacker's punching hand.

When the punch comes towards you, rotate your hand so that the palm is facing towards you. As you do this, ensure there is a slight lead with your elbow so you can make contact with the punch as soon as possible.

Once your arm makes contact with the punch, redirect the line of the punch away from your body by continuing to sweep your arm across your midsection as you perform a slight rotation with your body.

If the height of the punch is lower than your arm, you may have to do a slight crunch to ensure your arm is low enough to intercept the blow before it strikes you.

Recoil your arm to prepare to deliver a counterstrike or defend the next attack.

# CHAPTER 9

# CHOKE & HEADLOCK DEFENSES

## Choke Defenses

In this scenario, we are defending a stationary choke or a choke in which the victim remains in place and is not being pushed or pulled. It is a static scenario where the attacker is just choking the victim in place.

### Choke from the Front – 2 Handed Pluck

To defend against this attack, you need to first address the immediate danger. In this instance, the immediate danger is the hands of the attacker performing the choke, making it hard to breathe.

Begin this defense by first using your hands to aggressively pluck the hands of the attacker. This builds on our natural reaction to grab at the attacker's hands. However, we will modify the grab to make it more effective. To pluck, make hooks with your hands and send them in between the hands of the attacker, ensuring your hands are deep into the attacker's hands so that you are plucking at the attacker's thumbs.

Maintain the hooks with your hands and aggressively pluck out using your entire upper body. By using your upper body, you are using all the muscles in your back, shoulders, and arms to defend against the attacker's thumbs, the weakest part of his grip. This helps a smaller, weaker person successfully defend a choke from a larger, stronger attacker.

Deliver a front kick to the attacker's groin at the same time you are plucking the attacker's hands off your throat.

After you have plucked the hands and delivered the kick, neutralize the attacker with continued counterattacks, such as a punch or elbow.

### Choke from the front – 1 Handed Pluck

In this scenario, we are defending a stationary choke, just as we did with the two-handed pluck. However, in this situation, we will look at an alternative way to defend and counter the attack if, for whatever reason, we may not be able to use both hands immediately. An example would be that maybe you were holding something in your hand and had to let go before you were able to use it. There would be no sense in delaying the other hand as it is free to start the defense, so you can begin with one and immediately bring the other hand into the defense once it is free.

To do this particular defense, just as with the two-handed pluck, you will have to address the immediate danger, which is the hands of the attacker choking you. To defend against this choke, you will still pluck aggressively in the same manner as you did with the two-hand pluck, but this time, you will only use one of your hands (the hand that is free). To pluck, make the hook with the plucking hand and pluck one of the attacker's hands, ensuring your hand is deep into the attacker's hand so that you are plucking at the attacker's thumbs.

As you pluck with one hand, the other hand will come up between the attacker's arms to deliver a palm strike to the face.

Immediately after the strike, begin delivering more counterattacks, such as knees, in order to neutralize the attacker.

## *Choke from the Side*

There may be a time when the attacker comes up to you from the side and places his hands around your neck to choke you. In this situation, you are at a slight disadvantage because you don't have all of your weapons available to you due to the angle of the attacker in relation to your body. However, you can use the same tactic you used with the one-handed pluck – defend the choke with one hand and counterattack with the other.

In this particular scenario, let's assume the attacker is on your right side. As he chokes you, reach up and over your right shoulder, using your left hand. Then, use

the same pluck defense as you did with the front chokes. As you make the hook with your hand, pluck down aggressively across your chest, making contact with the attacker's hand.

It is crucial that you reach beyond the attacker's hand and your neck, and then pluck down. This action will allow you to build the momentum you need to successfully pluck the hands and relieve the pressure on your neck.

As you pluck, use your right hand and deliver a strike to the attacker's groin. It doesn't matter if you strike with a fist or palm strike, as long as you produce a solid blow. (I prefer the palm strike as it covers a greater surface area and provides an increased chance of striking my intended target, but the fist will work fine as well.)

As you deliver the strike, shift the weight of your body towards the attacker to put more force into the hit. If the attacker is too close, strike as best you can, forcing them back to create enough space for a second, more powerful strike.

Once you've plucked the hand and delivered the groin strike, the natural reaction of the attacker is then to double over. As he does, aggressively raise your right elbow up to strike the attacker's chin. Ensure you drive through your target to maximize your strike. (Note: the attacker may not always respond by doubling over. If this is the case, you can improvise using various other strikes).

At this point, you have addressed the immediate danger and delivered a simultaneous counterattack and can now turn to face the attacker. As you turn, deliver a hammerfist to the side and continue with more strikes once you are facing the attacker.

Neutralize your attacker through the continuation of strikes.

## Choke from Behind

Any situation where the attacker attacks you from behind, you are at a disadvantage. So, in the situation the attacker is choking you from behind, we will address the immediate danger and then position ourselves into a much more advantageous position as we counterattack.

As with all the chokes we've covered thus far, we are going to deal with the immediate danger by using the pluck to address the pressure the attacker is putting on our throat. To do this pluck, reach as far back behind your head as possible using both of your hands. Your elbows should point forward, and you should lower your chin to your chest to help you reach further.

If you happen to reach far enough back that you gouge the attacker's eyes or scratch his face in the process, then it is a bonus.

What you should be reaching for is the weakest part of the attacker's grip, which, as in all our choke scenarios above, is the thumbs. Once your hands are as far back as possible, pluck forward, making contact with the attacker's thumbs and then aggressively down and towards your chest.

As you pluck and break the choke, you should be stepping back and to the side of the attacker so you can get out from in front of him and into a position so you can begin to turn towards him and deliver counters. It doesn't matter which side you step back towards, as either one will work. Just know that your tactical situation can dictate to which side you move. In this example, we will assume you step to the left and back.

Once you have broken the choke and as you are stepping back and to the side of the attacker, you should let go of the attacker's hands with the arm that is closer to the attacker. In this example, it will be your right hand. As you let go, your natural momentum from the downward pluck wants to continue moving your arm downward. So, capitalize on this movement and use the downward motion of your arm to strike the groin of the attacker. Use an open hand as you strike since this covers more surface area. Use your left hand to maintain control of the attacker's left hand.

Once you have delivered the groin strike, recoil your right hand and then deliver a right elbow to the attacker's face, continuing to hold the attacker's left hand with your left hand.

After you have delivered an elbow, then deliver a right side hammerfist to the attacker. As you deliver the hammerfist, turn in toward the attacker to face him. As you do this, let go of the attacker's left hand.

Be sure as you turn toward the attacker that you move your right leg around the attacker's leg, so you don't trip during the turn.

At this point, you will be facing the attacker. Continue with multiple counterattacks, neutralizing your attacker.

## Choke from the Front with a Push

Attackers will not always execute a choke from a stationary position. In fact, chokes with a push may be more commonplace from an aggressive attacker. When an attacker pushes and chokes you at the same time, you have to change your initial response to address a different immediate danger: that of being forced off balance.

So, let's look at the first scenario, where an attacker is choking and pushing you from the front. Again, the immediate danger is the push. So to deal with this, we first have to ensure we don't get pushed off balance. When you feel the push backward, you have to step back and base out on one foot.

It doesn't matter which foot you base on, but as a recommendation, you should train on both sides. To describe the technique, we will assume you base on your right foot. As you base out on your right foot, stab your left hand into the air with your bicep as close to your ear as possible to trap the attacker's hands between your arm and head.

Now, as we gain control over the attack, you turn your head to the right to break the attacker's grip on your neck to address the choke itself.

At this point, we have dealt with the choke, so now we need to clear the attacker's hands off our neck to finish the defense. To do that, drive your left elbow down to clear the attacker's arms while simultaneously bringing your right hand up to catch and trap his hands.

Now that we have control over the attacker, we can begin throwing counterattacks. A good one to use from this position is a side elbow strike (elbow #2) and follow up with knees, kicks, and other strikes to neutralize the attacker.

## Choke from Behind with a Push

Now, let's look at the second scenario, where an attacker is choking and pushing you from behind. Again, the immediate danger is the push.

And, just as we did with the choke from the front with a push, with the choke from behind with a push, we have to ensure we don't get taken off balance. To help you catch yourself and recover from the push, when you feel the push forward, you have to step forward and base out on one foot. It doesn't matter which foot you base on, but as a recommendation, you should train on both sides. To describe the technique, we will assume you base on your left foot.

As you base out on your left foot, stab your right hand into the air with your bicep as close to your ear as possible to trap the attacker's hands between your arm and head. For training purposes, think of shooting your hand out the top of your head.

Now, as we gain control over the attack, sharply rotate your upper torso and head to the right to break the attacker's grip on your neck and step back with your right foot as your momentum continues to carry you forward.

Rotate sharply and step back, breaking the attacker's grip. Then clear his hands off your neck by driving your right elbow down and catching the attacker's hands and arm with your upper arm. At this point, you can begin delivering multiple counters to the attacker, such as a punch, kick, elbow, or knee.

# Headlock from Behind

Another form of possible attack from an assailant is the headlock from behind. There are multiple variations of this, such as the bar arm, or carotid choke. The difference is the objective for each. The bar arm headlock is meant to be a choke that compromises, or cuts off, your breathing. With the carotid headlock, the primary purpose is to cut off the blood flow to your head, causing you to pass out. Regardless of the attack, the defense is very similar for both, but we'll look at each one individually.

## Bar Arm Headlock

With the bar arm headlock, the attacker's forearm is against the windpipe, attempting to crush it to cut off your air flow.

Our natural reaction in this instance is to pull at the arm so we can breathe. So, we are going to build on that instinctive movement to help us get out of this. As your hands come up, send them toward the attacker's hands (the open end of the headlock) and make hooks with your hands. Using the hooks, pluck at the attacker's hands, ensuring that you continually accelerate your movement.

As you pluck, turn your head and torso toward your hands and turn towards the attacker in a tight movement.

The pluck, combined with the rotation into the attacker, will allow you to create enough space in the attacker's headlock to turn into him. As you turn in toward the attacker, tuck your head and remove it out from under the attacker's arm.

As you remove your head from the hold, maintain control of the attacker's arm and use it to control and manipulate him while you deliver counter strikes.

## Carotid Headlock

With the carotid headlock, the attacker's forearm and bicep are used to restrict blood flow by exerting pressure against the carotid artery, with the bend in their elbow placed on the front of our throat. This results in the attacker applying pressure both sides of your neck, resulting in restricted blood flow to the head.

At this point, the defense for this is like what we did for the bar arm headlock. The major difference is that because of the positioning of the attacker's arm and hand, you will have to reach further back toward your shoulder to pluck at the attacker's hand(s). Additionally, since the lack of blood flow can cause you to pass out within seconds, you have a limited time to respond and must react quickly and effectively.

Our natural reaction is to pull at the arm so we build on this instinctive movement as we did with the bar arm headlock. As your hands come up, send them toward the attacker's hands (the open end of the headlock) and make hooks with your hands. Using the hooks, pluck at the attacker's hands, ensuring that you continually accelerate your movement.

As you pluck, turn your head and torso toward your hands and turn towards the attacker in a tight movement.

The pluck, combined with the rotation into the attacker, will allow you to create enough space in the attacker's headlock to turn into him. As you turn in toward the attacker, tuck your head and remove it out from under the attacker's arm.

As you remove your head from the hold, maintain control of the attacker's arm and use it to control and manipulate him while you deliver counter strikes.

# CHAPTER 10

# WRIST RELEASES

## Wrist Releases

Wrist releases, as presented here, are some of the softer techniques in Krav Maga. With these particular defenses, we assume the attacker is not being overly aggressive or trying to force or drag you somewhere. If this were the case, you would burst in and attack. Instead, in this milder scenario, the aggressor attacks with firmness but is not physically striking you or being overly aggressive. Therefore, you would respond firmly, but not necessarily in a full out assault on them.

When working with wrist releases, one of the key points to remember is that the weakest part of the grip is the thumb. To capitalize on this, we are going to leverage against the thumb to disengage our wrists from the aggressor's grip. Remember, these concepts apply to a variety of wrist grab scenarios, but we will only cover a few basic, more common types of wrist grabs.

### *Wrist Release – Same Side Grab*
When the attacker grabs your wrist using the same side (his left grabbing your right), again, you want to leverage the grip at the thumb.

To do this, drive the elbow of the wrist that has been grabbed toward his elbow as if you were going to strike it while moving your wrist against the attacker's thumb.

In doing this, your wrist will gain the leverage it needs to break free of the attacker's grip. At this point, your hands should come up and you should end in a fight stance in case the attacker decides to escalate.

## Wrist Release – Opposite Side Grab

In this scenario, the attacker grabs your wrist on the opposite side of his arm (his left grabbing your left).

To get free of this grab, drive your elbow up towards his and move your wrist against the attacker's thumb. You can think of this movement as similar to a hitchhiking motion with your hand. However, you should remember to drive your elbow toward the attacker and not pull away.

As you complete the release, your hands should come up, and you should end in a fight stance.

## Two Hands Held Low

When the attacker grabs both wrists with each of his hands, the situation is starting to escalate with the attacker becoming more aggressive in his attempts to control you. In this particular instance, the attacker is holding both of your hands down, with his thumbs toward the inside of his arms.

Since we are going against the thumbs to break his grip, we will simultaneously bring each wrist inside and up, while also driving both elbows up toward the attacker's arms.

After the release, ensure your hands stay up and you are in a fight stance.

As a side note, if you feel the attacker is quickly escalating to a more aggressive posture, as soon as you perform the release you can do a quick shove to create space and get out of the situation or continue with more strikes. Doing so is a decision you have to make in the moment based on your perception of the attacker's mindset.

## Two Hands Held High

As in the above scenario, when the attacker grabs both wrists with each of his hands, the situation is starting to escalate. However, in this particular instance, the attacker is holding both of your hands up, and with his thumbs toward the inside of his arms.

Since we are going against the thumbs to break his grip, we will simultaneously drive each wrist inside and down, essentially making a circular movement down and in.

Your wrists should break free of the grip towards the lower part of the movement, and you should immediately bring your hands up to protect your face while you move into a fight stance.

And, just like in the hand held low wrist release, if you feel the attacker is quickly escalating to a more aggressive posture, as soon as you perform the release you can do a quick shove to create space and get out of the situation or continue with more strikes.

## Two Handed Grab

Sometimes the attacker may grab one wrist with both of his hands.

To defend this type of grab, the defender should make a fist with the hand that is being held while reaching with the other hand to grab their fist between the attacker's arms.

Once you grab your fist with your opposite hand, pull back on t it while driving the elbow of the arm being held toward the attacker's elbow, similar to the defense you did for the same side grab.

By using leverage from your arm against the attacker's hands, you can successfully free yourself from this grip.

Once you have freed your arm from their grip, you should be in a fight stance ready to defend or deliver strikes.

Please note that the two-handed grab is a more aggressive attack and may require the defender to be more aggressive with their defense than they were in the other wrist releases.

# CHAPTER 11

# FALL BREAKS

## Fall Breaks

In Krav Maga, while our goal is to ensure we stay on our feet, there may be times where we lose our balance or get tripped and fall to the ground. It is crucial to ensure we fall to the ground in such a way to minimize the damage we take and to allow us to stay in the fight and defend ourselves from the ground.

We will look at two scenarios where we are falling either on our back or our side. The key focus in either situation is to eliminate or minimize the impact on our spine and our head, as well as ensuring we don't break any limbs in the process.

### *Fall Break - Back*

To perform a back fall break, you want to ensure you first tuck your chin into your chest as you are falling to minimize the impact of your head on the ground.

As you do this, you should land on your shoulder/upper back as much as possible while extending your arms out at an angle. By using the arms and upper back, we disperse the force of the impact across a larger surface area and reduce the amount of impact we take on the back alone.

Ideally, you want your arms to impact the ground at the same time as your upper back. To help you do this, think of slapping the ground at the same time your back lands.

Immediately go to your ground fighting position (covered in Chapter 11) once you have landed on the ground with your arms helping to absorb the impact

## Fall Break – Side

The principle is the same to perform the side fall break - absorb the impact of the fall by dispersing it across a larger surface area by using your arm and upper body.

However, in this instance, we can only use one of our arms.

Just as in the back fall break, you want to land towards the upper side of your body to avoid injury to the lower rib cage. As you do this, use the arm that is on the same side as you are falling to reach out at an acute angle (less than 90 degrees) to the body and, again, slap the ground as your side makes an impact. When falling, ensure your head is held up to avoid hitting it on the ground.

Immediately go to your side ground fight position (Chapter 11) once you have done this and safely fallen to the ground.

# CHAPTER 12

# GROUND POSITIONS & KICKS

## Ground Positions

In Krav Maga, our goal is never to wind up on the ground. However, there may be times when we do. In that instance, we have ways of dealing with the attacker, whether they are standing or on the ground with us. In this section, we will discuss what to do when the attacker is standing and you are on the ground.

The first concept we will look at is the basic positions we have for when we end up on the ground – the back and side positions. Additionally, we'll consider the movement capabilities we have in each position.

### *Back position*

As mentioned in the previous section, we can end up in the back position when we first get to the ground and perform a fall break. At that moment, we will go to our back ground position allowing us the opportunity to defend and counter against an attacker that is standing and is continuing to attacking us.

In this ground position you need to keep your hands up in the same manner as when you are in your standing fight stance, ensuring you keep your head off the ground.

Place one foot flat on the ground, keeping it as close to your body as possible.

Ensure you chamber the other foot with the knee close to the chest, and the toes pointed up with the bottom of the foot facing the attacker.

## Movement in back position

When you are in the back position, you have the ability to move until you are able to get into a position where you can safely stand up. Remember, you have one foot on the ground as your base foot with the other leg chambered, and the foot facing your attacker.

If the attacker moves, you move with him. You should be able to push off your base foot in the direction the attacker is moving, ensuring you keep your chambered foot trained on the attacker. This gives you the opportunity to use a kick against him if he tries to come in towards you.

If the attacker moves to the right, pivot your body to keep your foot in line with him. Note that the foot facing the attacker depends on which side of your body's centerline the attacker is on. For instance, when the attacker is to the left of your centerline, your left foot should be up and the right foot down. If the attacker is to the right of your centerline, then your right foot should be up and the left foot down.

You should always be moving in the ground position to keep up with your attacker's movement. As soon as he is right of your centerline, lift your right foot up and, as he moves to the right, pivot on your back in the same direction.

If he is on the left side of your centerline, do the same thing, but with the left foot up and pivoting to the left.

As soon as he crosses the centerline, you change which foot you have up, based on the side he is on.

One thing to keep in mind is that the foot you keep up as your weapon does not depend as much on the direction the attacker is moving. The main determinant is the position of the attacker relative to you, regardless of his motion.

## Side Position

When you are in a situation where you perform the side fall break, you will end up in a side ground position. Once you have done the side fall break, you should immediately come up on your forearm or hand, using the arm that is on the ground. The other hand should immediately come up in front of your face to protect it.

Just like in the back position, we will use one leg as a base leg, and the other will be the weapon. The side you land on will determine which leg does which task. For instance, if you land on your right side, your right side will be your base leg and the left leg will be chambered so you can use it as the kicking leg. If you land on the left side, it will be opposite.

It is essential to keep your base leg tucked in tight to your body for stability and also to keep the attacker from stomping on your leg.

## Movement

Movement in the side position follows the same concept of the centerline that we used in the back position. However, to change which leg is the kicking leg will require you to flip over quickly to keep up with the attacker. To demonstrate this, assume you are on your right side, so your left leg is your kicking leg. The attacker is directly on your centerline, so you are in the perfect position to attack him if need be. If the attacker moves right, you will pivot on your hip and leg, using the hand or forearm to push and guide you as you keep your foot trained on the attacker.

But, when the attacker changes direction to move to your left and crosses your centerline, you have to react to ensure he does not get behind you. At the point when he crosses the centerline, quickly roll back to your left, switching your feet so that the left leg now becomes the base leg and your right leg becomes the kicking leg. And, of course, your left forearm or hand is now your base, while the right hand comes up to protect your face.

If the attacker continues to stay on the left of your centerline, you stay on your left side and pivot to keep up with him. And, just as with moving in the back position, it's not the direction the attacker is moving, but the attacker's position that determines which side you are on.

## Kicks from the ground

When we are on the ground in the back or side positions, we have options for not only defending, but for striking the attacker. The best weapons we have in this instance are our legs and feet. In our ground positions, we have our leg chambered to give us the best possible offensive weapon. Depending on the position we are in, we have some basic kicks we can use.

### *Front Kick*

The front kick can be used in either position. To attack using the front kick, we want to kick just as we did when standing up, using the defensive front kick. If you remember, we used our hips driving forward in the kick to increase the power and effectiveness of our strike. We use that exact same concept with the front kick on the ground. From the back position, we will engage the hips for the kick by rolling back onto our shoulders as we lift our hips off the ground using the base foot.

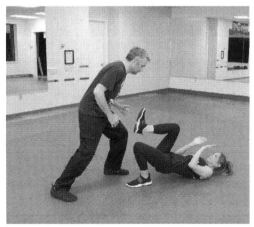

As we do this, we extend the kicking leg out forcefully to "stomp" the attacker, just like we did when we were standing.

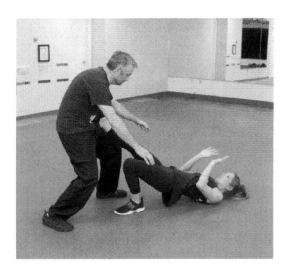

All these things should happen at the same time – roll back to shoulders, raise hips, kick with leg – while we maintain our hands in front of our face. Then, once the kick has done its job, we recoil and return to our back position.

As an important safety note, ensure that you do not kick too soon, as you run the risk of hyperextending your knee. Make sure the attacker is close enough for you to connect this kick solidly.

### Round Kick

You can use the round kick in either ground position, but for this description, we will focus on the doing the round kick from the back. It is done similarly from the side position. The round kick is ideal for a situation when the attacker is able to get past your initial defenses and moves closer to you while you're on the ground. The round kick works well because the attacker is a little closer to you and you now have the option of using your shin to strike as well as the foot.

In this scenario, we will assume, the attacker is moving to the right of your centerline, which means your right foot should be up and the left foot is the base foot.

As the attacker moves in towards you, push off your base foot with the left foot, and, with a quick switching movement, roll your right hip over and snap your left leg out from the knee, driving with the shin or foot of your leg, striking your target. Typically, the knee or lower leg is the best option, but strike any target that presents itself.

Immediately go to a side or back position to be ready to defend and counter again, once you've kicked the target. If you have the opportunity, get up into a standing position. Be careful, though, as this may not always be possible, in which case, it is better to stay on the ground.

## Side Kick

Use the side kick from the side ground position. Just like the front kick on the ground, the side kick will require us to use our hips to maximize the power of the kick. Assuming you are on the right side with your right leg as your base leg and your left leg chambered, raise your hips off the ground, using your right arm or hand to balance yourself while keeping the left hand in front of your face to protect it.

At the same time, you will explosively deliver a side kick with the left leg, ensuring your foot is parallel to the ground and striking the target with your heel.

Immediately return to a side or back position once you strike your target unless you have an opportunity to get up.

## *Getting up from the Ground*

While we know how to defend ourselves on the ground, our ultimate goal is to get on our feet. The longer we are on the ground, the more disadvantageous the position becomes, particularly if we are dealing with multiple attackers. So, we need to have a way to quickly and efficiently get up back to our standing position so we can be ready for any further attacks or to get out of the situation altogether.

In preparing ourselves to get up in a fight, we first need to ensure that we do have the opportunity to do so. If we try to get up but have an attacker standing to close in front of us, we risk another attack while we are in the middle of getting up.

If we don't give ourselves the proper space and timing, we risk being taken back down to the ground and may wind up in a worse position or sustain a worse injury. There is no hard and fast rule about how far away the attacker should be before you try to get up. That is something you will have to determine based on your capabilities and training, as well as what you can assess in the moment of the fight.

Now, to get up from the ground, we are first going to start from the back position on the ground. In this scenario, we will assume your left foot is the base foot and the right foot is up and chambered as your kicking foot.

To begin getting up, you will roll to the side where your leg is up, in this instance the right side. As you roll, place your right hand on the ground. It is important to keep your foot positioning the same, with your right foot off the ground and left foot on the ground.

Once you are in this position, push with your base hand, while keeping your other hand in front of your face to protect it. As you push off with your hand, your hips should come off the ground. At this point, you should have two points of contact on the ground – your right hand and left foot in this scenario.

Now, swing your right foot back so that it ends up going past your right hand and place that foot on the ground. At this point, your right hand should still be on the ground between your legs as you get ready to stand with your left hand still protecting your face.

From this modified squat position, stand up into your fight stance, staying alert and prepared to continue fighting or escape the situation, whichever action is required.

*Optional method:* If you have problems using only one hand to lift yourself off the ground you can put both hands on the ground to balance yourself. Using the same process described above, roll to your side and place both hands on the ground.

Once both hands are on the ground, swing your right leg back until it passes your right hand and then stand up in into your fight stance.

Be aware, though, that because you used both hands to help lift yourself up, you have exposed your head to strikes, so it is imperative you stand up quickly and, as soon as possible, get your hands back up into a fight stance.

CHAPTER 13

# HANDGUN DEFENSES

## Handgun Defenses

When an attacker confronts you with a firearm, the situation suddenly becomes a lot more dangerous. Unlike a choke or headlock where you can afford to do something incorrectly in your defense and still recover, if your attacker has a gun and you do something wrong, the gun could go off and injure or kill you or someone else. So, it becomes even more important in your training to pay attention to the details of what you are doing to ensure your best chance of survival. When you are defending an attacker with a gun, you should apply four basic principles to defend yourself against that weapon: redirect the line of fire, control the weapon, counterattack, and disarm.

*Principle 1*: Redirecting the line of fire ensures you are not in the path of the bullet if and when the gun goes off. And, remember, once you leave the line of fire, you never go back into it. There are numerous ways to redirect depending on the placement of the gun, where it is in relation to you or someone else, and how they are holding the weapon. One thing you should remember, though, is that you try to redirect the weapon the shortest distance off your body. For instance, if there's a gun aimed at the right side of your chest, you want to redirect the weapon to the right, as it will get your body out of the line of fire faster than if you redirect it to the left, especially since moving the gun to the left crosses over a vital organ.

Additionally, when redirecting, you should use the concept of least detectable motion. When an attacker has a gun pointed at me, any movement he sees, may alert him to my intentions and entice him to go ahead and shoot before I ever have the chance to reach the weapon. If we use the visibly perceived smallest amount of movement possible, we improve our chances of redirecting that weapon before the gunman can fire at us.

*Principle 2*: Controlling the weapon is vital to making sure you do not get back in the line of fire. Controlling the gun is the step where you begin to take control from the attacker and shift the advantage to you. It also gives you the opportunity to move to the next two phases of the defense, the counterattack and disarm.

*Principle 3*: Counterattacking gives you the chance to distract the attacker, preferably with as much pain as possible, giving them something else to focus on other than the gun. And, if done right, you can take the fight out of your attacker, further ensuring you defend yourself. How many strikes should you use during the counterattack phase? The best option is to strike enough to distract and temporarily weaken the gunman, but you always want to get two hands on the weapon and disarm as soon as possible. The longer you fight over the weapon without 100% control of it, the higher the risk you can get shot.

*Principle 4*: Disarming the attacker is the final phase of the gun defense. Once you have control of the weapon, you can now leverage the opportunity to disengage and get away from the situation without being shot. If you are carrying your own firearm, this is the point at which you can safely draw your weapon. You have the option to use the attacker's weapon against him if you need to, but use caution as you do not know the gun you took from the attacker. It may be functioning well, or it may not be. Additionally, you have to take into account the laws of the state you are in. The best and safest option is to get out of the situation if you can.

These four basic principles will usually be applied in this order, though there are a few situations where we may switch out the counterattack and disarm (we will cover those later in the system). In this level, we will focus on two basic gun scenarios that successfully demonstrate the application of these principles.

## Gun from the front

In this scenario, a gunman is standing in front of you with the gun pointed directly at you, holding it with one hand (we'll assume the right hand in this example). For now, we will assume the gun is aimed at the center of your chest or slightly to the right of center.

As mentioned earlier, we want to redirect the line of fire. To accomplish this, we want to use our left hand to redirect the gun to our right. Bring your left hand up using the least detectable motion possible. To help you move in a way that is imperceptible to the attacker, think of keeping your arm close to your body as you raise your arm up. If there were a bright light behind you, the attacker should not be able to see light between your arm and your body. This keeps your arm moving in a vertical plane until the moment that it reaches the gun, making your movement less detectable by the attacker.

When your hand reaches the weapon, make contact with the weapon by making an L shape with your thumb and index finger and rotate your hand so that you catch the gun in the webbing between those fingers.

Maintain contact between your hand and the gun as you move the gun directly to your right until the line of fire is off your body.

As you move the gun off your body, wrap your fingers around the weapon.

Once the weapon is off your body and you are out of the line of fire drive the gun towards the attacker. To do this, think of trying to punch towards the attacker's midsection, driving the gun into the area around his belt buckle, just to the left of where it would be. It is also beneficial to point the gun in a slight downward direction while it is pinned to the attacker. This helps keep the gun from firing at someone else.

As you do this, burst in with your body slightly bladed and stepping toward the shoulder of the arm holding the weapon. Ideally, you should wind up with your right hip in front of his right hip. By lining up your right hip in front of his, you create a larger angle for him to rotate the gun if he wants to point it at you again.

To help keep the gun against the body, you need to ensure you keep your weight on the gun and press it into the body of the attacker.

Make sure you are not too far away or too close to successfully do this. If you are too far away, you will lose some of the control you are trying to gain.

If you are too close, you run the risk of him being able to deliver close range counters, such as head butt or elbows. Also, if you are too close, he can effectively push you back, which may buy him the opportunity to put you back in the line of fire.

*Too far*          *Too close*

Once you burst in and gain control of the weapon by pinning it against his body, deliver a counterattack using a punch to the face.

You can punch one or two times to the face, but any more than that and you risk the gunman regaining control. So, it is best to only deliver one or two strikes as you want to put two hands on the weapon as quickly as possible.

After your punch, immediately recoil your punch while maintaining control and keeping the weapon pinned on this body. If the attacker stumbles or falls back, you stay on him. If he goes to the ground, you keep the weapon on his body.

As soon as you recoil your punch, use the punching hand (in this example the right hand) and follow down the path of the left arm until you reach the gun. If you use the arm as a guide to the gun, you remove the guesswork of where it is. You know it is at the end of your arm, so follow it there.

When your hand reaches the gun, reach your right hand underneath the gun with your palm up, and grab the butt of the gun.

At this point, you will have two hands on the firearm and an increased amount of control over it. Once you have that control, you immediately begin the disarm. To take the gun away, you will sharply rotate the gun by rotating the weapon abruptly toward the attacker. The hand on the barrel rotates the barrel toward the attacker.

At the same time, using the hand that is covering the butt of the weapon, pull the gun towards you.

Doing this gives you a push-pull rotational movement of the gun, snapping it in the grip of the attacker. If the gunman's finger is on the trigger, this will cause some pain for him as it rotates the finger in the trigger guard and places severe, quick pain on the finger.

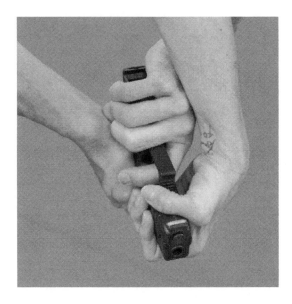

Once you've done the rotation, pull the gun towards you with the barrel continuing to point toward the attacker and away from you. While keeping both hands on the weapon, pull your hands and the gun into your hip.

By doing this, it is my signal that it is now safe to move away from the attacker and disengage. If you move prematurely and have not succeeded in relieving the attacker of his weapon, you risk putting yourself back in the line of fire. But, if you wait until you feel it in your hip, you have a signal that you are safe to disengage and start putting distance between you and the attacker.

As you disengage, if possible, you want to exit at an angle and in such a way that makes it more difficult for the attacker to come towards you. Any direction that forces the attacker to turn and change his angle of approach is desirable. However, if you can only move straight back, then move that direction.

As a final note, you may have to continue counterattacks if the attacker continues to come towards you. If you have a gun of your own, you can now draw it and use it to

control any further movement of the attacker which is especially useful for law enforcement once they disarm their subject and need to use their sidearm.

## Gun to the head - front

For a gun aimed at your head, you perform the same defense. However, as you redirect the weapon away from your head, you would move your head in the opposite direction you are taking the gun.

You must ensure you don't move your head first as this may alert the attacker and he may pull the trigger. If you are fast enough, you may be able to avoid being shot, but if you're not, you run the risk of taking a bullet to the head. If you wait to move your head until your redirecting hand has made contact with the gun, then you can have a simultaneous movement of the weapon going one way while your head goes the other.

After that, perform the defense the same way you did as the regular gun from the front.

## Gun to the head – side

When the attacker has the gun pointed to the side of your head, the concepts are still the same; we change the initial redirection of the technique and the head movement.

In this example, we will assume the gunman is right-handed and is on your left side holding the gun to the left side of your head in front of the ear. If the gun is behind the ear, it would change our technique (which is covered in other levels). As a note, you can do this technique on different sides with the gunman using a different hand. but the explanation is more straightforward if we assume these basic conditions. To be good in all situations, you should always train multiple sides using a left and right-handed shooter.

When the gunman first puts the gun to your head, just like with gun to the head from the front, you want to ensure your head gets out of the line of fire at the same time you are redirecting the weapon. To accomplish this, we want to use the hand that is closest to the gun to do the redirection. In our example, we would use the left side.

Remember, we want to use the least detectable motion when reaching for the weapon, so we will bring the right hand up along our side to the weapon with the palm facing out away from us. Try to bring the hand up in a straight line, avoiding an outward, circular movement. The outward circular motion is a significant enough movement for the gunman to see and respond to, while a straight line movement directly up to the weapon is minimal in comparison.

Once your hand reaches the gun, with the palm out, grab the gun around the barrel and push it out away from your head. Simultaneously, you will move your head back, as if you are pulling your chin back into your neck.

At this point, you have successfully redirected the weapon and are now ready to move into the control portion of the technique. Maintain control of the weapon with the hand that redirected it and turn in to the attacker.

Now you are in the same position you were when you defended the gun from the front. So continue the same way you did in that defense, with the hand driving toward the attacker's body and pinning the gun to his midsection.

Then you would counter with a punch to the attacker's face using your right hand.

Perform the recoil and follow the length of the arm to the gun and grab the butt of the weapon by going underneath it and capping it with the palm facing up.

Sharply rotate the gun by pulling the right hand toward you and the left hand rotating toward the attacker, breaking the attacker's grip. Pull the weapon towards your right hip removing it from the attacker's hands.

Once you feel the gun in your hip, disengage and move out at an angle, continuing to counterattack if needed. Or, if you have your own gun, you would draw it at this time.

# Final Notes

This concludes the yellow belt portion of the Krav Maga curriculum at Krav Fit. As with anything, regular practice will make you better at these techniques. When you train, make sure you train the technical aspects of the techniques so you can be better and move faster. The more technically sound, the faster you will become. While we don't say you have to be perfect in each technique, the better you are, the more proficient at defending yourself you will be. As you train, you should also train under stress and in various conditions to simulate the unpredictability of a live attack. You should always be prepared to defend yourself, but you should also be ready to adapt to the situation you are in. For instance, are there barriers or are you in a crowd of people. Is it a low level of light, is there a lot of noise? And, you should train with the attacker coming at you left handed and right handed, left side and right side. And, in the same way, you should train to defend and counter with your left and right side. While we can never adequately prepare to defend all situations 100%, we can be prepared to adapt quickly and respond effectively.

Additionally, you should strive to improve your level of fitness. While you don't have to be in shape to effectively defend yourself, it can help you survive an encounter. The longer you can outlast your attacker, the better your chances of going home safe. You should always do what you can to improve your chances in a fight.

So, continue your training, train aggressively, and train in a variety of situations against a variety of attackers. All while striving to improve your level of fitness. In this way, you'll continue to improve your response time, your skills, and your reaction to a violent attack.

Have fun training, learn a lot, and take control!

# ABOUT THE AUTHOR

Devin has been training in Krav Maga since 2001 and is currently a 3$^{rd}$ degree Black Belt in Krav Maga. He also has experience and training in kickboxing, Japanese Jiu Jitsu, Brazilian Jiu Jitsu, and is a certified Israeli Tactical Knife Instructor, Krav Maga instructor, and Krav Maga Law Enforcement instructor. Additionally, he has experience in boxing, wrestling, and military hand to hand combat. Devin is a member of the Israeli Federation of Martial Arts (IFMA) and a member and instructor recognized by the Federation of Israeli Martial Arts (FIMA). He is a 1996 graduate of the United States Military Academy at West Point, and served in the U.S. Army. Devin is President and founder of Krav Fit, which serves to license and certify those wishing to train in and teach the Krav Maga system.

Made in the USA
Las Vegas, NV
19 November 2020

11047434R00081